This Book Belongs To:

Copyright 2019

All rights reserved. No part of this publication may be reproduced, stored in a retrieval system, or transmitted in any form or by any means, electronic, mechanical, photocopying, recording or otherwise, without the prior written permission of the publisher.

"THE MORE YOU LEARN, THE MORE YOU EARN"

Yearly Summary

Year_____

Summary	Budgeted	Actual
Income		
Bill Expenses		
Other Expenses		
Savings		
Total		

January	
Income	
Bill Expenses	
Other Expenses	
Savings	
Total	

February	
Income	
Bill Expenses	
Other Expenses	
Savings	
Total	

March	
Income	
Bill Expenses	
Other Expenses	
Savings	
Total	

April	
Income	
Bill Expenses	
Other Expenses	
Savings	
Total	

May	
Income	
Bill Expenses	
Other Expenses	
Savings	
Total	

June	
Income	
Bill Expenses	
Other Expenses	
Savings	
Total	

July	
Income	
Bill Expenses	
Other Expenses	
Savings	
Total	

August	
Income	
Bill Expenses	
Other Expenses	
Savings	
Total	

September	
Income	
Bill Expenses	
Other Expenses	
Savings	
Total	

October	
Income	
Bill Expenses	
Other Expenses	
Savings	
Total	

November	
Income	
Bill Expenses	
Other Expenses	
Savings	
Total	

December	
Income	
Bill Expenses	
Other Expenses	
Savings	
Total	

Account Tracker

Account Name/Number_____ **Starting Balance**_____

Date	Transaction	Withdrawal	Deposit	Balance

Account Tracker

Account Name/Number_____ **Starting Balance**_____

Date	Transaction	Withdrawal	Deposit	Balance

Saving Tracker

Savings Goal _____ **Starting Balance** _____

Date	Description	Withdrawal	Deposit	Balance

Saving Tracker

Savings Goal _____ **Starting Balance** _____

Date	Description	Withdrawal	Deposit	Balance

Debt Payment Log

Creditor_____

Account No.		Interest Rate	
Target Payoff Date		Credit Limit	
Account Holder		Minimum Payment	
Credit Type		Starting Balance	
Account No.		Interest Rate	

Date	Payment made	Balance

Debt Payment Log

Creditor _____

Account No.		**Interest Rate**	
Target Payoff Date		**Credit Limit**	
Account Holder		**Minimum Payment**	
Credit Type		**Starting Balance**	
Account No.		**Interest Rate**	

Date	Payment made	Balance

Check Log

Check	Date	Description	Withdrawal	Deposit	Balance

Weekly Expense Tracker

Total Expenses : _____   **Balance :** _____

Friday
Date ……../………../……..

Description	Amount
Total	

Saturday
Date ……../……….../……..

Description	Amount
Total	

Sunday
Date ……../……….../……..

Description	Amount
Total	

Note

_____
_____
_____
_____
_____
_____
_____
_____
_____
_____
_____
_____

Weekly Expense Tracker

Week Of : **Month :** **Budget :**

Monday
Date ..../........./........

Description	Amount
Total	

Tuesday
Date ..../........./........

Description	Amount
Total	

Wednesday
Date ..../........./........

Description	Amount
Total	

Thursday
Date ..../........./........

Description	Amount
Total	

Weekly Expense Tracker

Total Expenses : _____   **Balance :** _____

Friday
Date ……./………/……..

Description	Amount
Total	

Saturday
Date ……./………/……..

Description	Amount
Total	

Sunday
Date ……./………/……..

Description	Amount
Total	

Note

_____
_____
_____
_____
_____
_____
_____
_____
_____
_____
_____
_____

Weekly Expense Tracker

Week Of : **Month :** **Budget :**

Monday
Date ..../.........../........

Description	Amount
Total	

Tuesday
Date ..../........../........

Description	Amount
Total	

Wednesday
Date ..../.........../........

Description	Amount
Total	

Thursday
Date ..../........./........

Description	Amount
Total	

Monthly Budget

Other Expenses	Date	Amount	Note
Total			

Total Income

Total Expenses

Difference

Notes

Weekly Expense Tracker

Week Of : _____   **Month :** _____   **Budget :** _____

Monday   Date ..../........./........

Description	Amount
Total	

Tuesday   Date ..../........./........

Description	Amount
Total	

Wednesday   Date ..../........./........

Description	Amount
Total	

Thursday   Date ..../........./........

Description	Amount
Total	

Weekly Expense Tracker

Total Expenses :   **Balance :**

Friday   Date ..../........./........

Description	Amount
Total	

Saturday   Date ..../........./........

Description	Amount
Total	

Sunday   Date ..../........./........

Description	Amount
Total	

Note

Weekly Expense Tracker

Week Of : **Month :** **Budget :**

Monday
Date ..../........../........

Description	Amount
Total	

Tuesday
Date ..../........../........

Description	Amount
Total	

Wednesday
Date ..../........../........

Description	Amount
Total	

Thursday
Date ..../........../........

Description	Amount
Total	

Weekly Expense Tracker

Total Expenses : _____   **Balance :** _____

Friday
Date ……../………../……..

Description	Amount
Total	

Saturday
Date ……../………../……..

Description	Amount
Total	

Sunday
Date ……../………../……..

Description	Amount
Total	

Note

Weekly Expense Tracker

Week Of : **Month :** **Budget :**

Monday   Date ……./……./…….

Description	Amount
Total	

Tuesday   Date ……./……./…….

Description	Amount
Total	

Wednesday   Date ……./……./…….

Description	Amount
Total	

Thursday   Date ……./……./…….

Description	Amount
Total	

Weekly Expense Tracker

Total Expenses : _____   **Balance :** _____

Friday   Date ……./……./…….

Description	Amount
Total	

Saturday   Date ……./……./…….

Description	Amount
Total	

Sunday   Date ……./……./…….

Description	Amount
Total	

Note

_____
_____
_____
_____
_____
_____
_____
_____
_____
_____
_____

Weekly Expense Tracker

Week Of :   **Month :**   **Budget :**

Monday
Date ..../........../........

Description	Amount
Total	

Tuesday
Date ..../........../........

Description	Amount
Total	

Wednesday
Date ..../........../........

Description	Amount
Total	

Thursday
Date ..../........../........

Description	Amount
Total	

Weekly Expense Tracker

Total Expenses : _____ **Balance :** _____

Friday Date ……../………./……..

Description	Amount
Total	

Saturday Date ……../………./……..

Description	Amount
Total	

Sunday Date ……../………./……..

Description	Amount
Total	

Note

_____
_____
_____
_____
_____
_____
_____
_____
_____
_____
_____

Weekly Expense Tracker

Week Of :   **Month :**   **Budget :**

Monday   Date ……../………../……..

Description	Amount
Total	

Tuesday   Date ……../……../…….

Description	Amount
Total	

Wednesday   Date ……../………../……..

Description	Amount
Total	

Thursday   Date ……../……../…….

Description	Amount
Total	

Weekly Expense Tracker

Total Expenses : _____   **Balance :** _____

Friday   Date ……../………./……..

Description	Amount
Total	

Saturday   Date ……../………./……..

Description	Amount
Total	

Sunday   Date ……../………./……..

Description	Amount
Total	

Note

_____
_____
_____
_____
_____
_____
_____
_____
_____
_____
_____

Monthly Budget

Income	
Income 1	
Income 2	
Other Income	
Total Income	

Budget :

Month :

Expenses

Bill To Be Paid	Date Due	Amount	Paid	Note
			○	
			○	
			○	
			○	
			○	
			○	
			○	
			○	
			○	
			○	
			○	
			○	
			○	
			○	
			○	
			○	
			○	
			○	
Total				

Monthly Budget

Other Expenses	Date	Amount	Note
Total			

Total Income

Total Expenses

Difference

Notes

Weekly Expense Tracker

Week Of :   **Month :**   **Budget :**

Monday
Date ……../………../……..

Description	Amount
Total	

Tuesday
Date ……../……../……..

Description	Amount
Total	

Wednesday
Date ……../………../……..

Description	Amount
Total	

Thursday
Date ……../……../……..

Description	Amount
Total	

Weekly Expense Tracker

Total Expenses :　　　　　　　　　**Balance :**

Friday　　　　　　　Date
…../…...../……..

Description	Amount
Total	

Saturday　　　　　　Date
……/……../……

Description	Amount
Total	

Sunday　　　　　　　Date
…../…...../……..

Description	Amount
Total	

Note

Weekly Expense Tracker

Week Of :   **Month :**   **Budget :**

Monday   Date ……../………../……..

Description	Amount
Total	

Tuesday   Date ……../………../……..

Description	Amount
Total	

Wednesday   Date ……../………../……..

Description	Amount
Total	

Thursday   Date ……../………../……..

Description	Amount
Total	

Weekly Expense Tracker

Total Expenses : _____   **Balance :** _____

Friday   Date ……/………/……..

Description	Amount
Total	

Saturday   Date ……/………/……..

Description	Amount
Total	

Sunday   Date ……/………/……..

Description	Amount
Total	

Note

_____
_____
_____
_____
_____
_____
_____
_____
_____
_____
_____

Weekly Expense Tracker

Week Of :　　　　　**Month :**　　　　　**Budget :**

Monday　　　Date ……./……../……..

Description	Amount
Total	

Tuesday　　　Date ……./……../……..

Description	Amount
Total	

Wednesday　　　Date ……./……../……..

Description	Amount
Total	

Thursday　　　Date ……./……../……..

Description	Amount
Total	

Weekly Expense Tracker

Total Expenses : _____   **Balance :** _____

Friday Date ……../………./……..

Description	Amount
Total	

Saturday Date ……../………./……..

Description	Amount
Total	

Sunday Date ……../………./……..

Description	Amount
Total	

Note

_____
_____
_____
_____
_____
_____
_____
_____
_____
_____
_____

Weekly Expense Tracker

Week Of : _____ **Month :** _____ **Budget :** _____

Monday
Date ……../………../………

Description	Amount
Total	

Tuesday
Date ……../………../………

Description	Amount
Total	

Wednesday
Date ……../………../………

Description	Amount
Total	

Thursday
Date ……../………../………

Description	Amount
Total	

Weekly Expense Tracker

Total Expenses : _____   **Balance :** _____

Friday   Date ……/………/……..

Description	Amount
Total	

Saturday   Date ……/………/……..

Description	Amount
Total	

Sunday   Date ……/………/……..

Description	Amount
Total	

Note

_____
_____
_____
_____
_____
_____
_____
_____
_____
_____
_____

Weekly Expense Tracker

Week Of : **Month :** **Budget :**

Monday
Date ..../........../........

Description	Amount
Total	

Tuesday
Date ..../........../........

Description	Amount
Total	

Wednesday
Date ..../........../........

Description	Amount
Total	

Thursday
Date ..../........../........

Description	Amount
Total	

Weekly Expense Tracker

Total Expenses : _____ **Balance :** _____

Friday Date ……/………../……..

Description	Amount
Total	

Saturday Date ……/……../……

Description	Amount
Total	

Sunday Date ……/………../……..

Description	Amount
Total	

Note

_____
_____
_____
_____
_____
_____
_____
_____
_____
_____

Monthly Budget

Income		
Income 1		
Income 2		
Other Income		
Total Income		

Budget :

Month :

Expenses

Bill To Be Paid	Date Due	Amount	Paid	Note
			○	
			○	
			○	
			○	
			○	
			○	
			○	
			○	
			○	
			○	
			○	
			○	
			○	
			○	
			○	
			○	
			○	
			○	
			○	
Total				

Monthly Budget

Other Expenses	Date	Amount	Note
Total			

Total Income

Total Expenses

Difference

Notes

Weekly Expense Tracker

Week Of : _____ **Month :** _____ **Budget :** _____

Monday — Date ……/……../……

Description	Amount
Total	

Tuesday — Date ……/……../……

Description	Amount
Total	

Wednesday — Date ……/……../……

Description	Amount
Total	

Thursday — Date ……/……../……

Description	Amount
Total	

Weekly Expense Tracker

Total Expenses : _____   **Balance :** _____

Friday
Date ……../………./……..

Description	Amount
Total	

Saturday
Date ……../………./……..

Description	Amount
Total	

Sunday
Date ……../………./……..

Description	Amount
Total	

Note

Weekly Expense Tracker

Week Of :   **Month :**   **Budget :**

Monday
Date ……../………../……..

Description	Amount
Total	

Tuesday
Date ……../………../……..

Description	Amount
Total	

Wednesday
Date ……../………../……..

Description	Amount
Total	

Thursday
Date ……../………../……..

Description	Amount
Total	

Weekly Expense Tracker

Total Expenses : _____   **Balance :** _____

Friday   Date ..../........./........

Description	Amount
Total	

Saturday   Date ..../........./........

Description	Amount
Total	

Sunday   Date ..../........./........

Description	Amount
Total	

Note

_____
_____
_____
_____
_____
_____
_____
_____
_____
_____
_____

Weekly Expense Tracker

Week Of :   **Month :**   **Budget :**

Monday   Date ..../........../........

Description	Amount
Total	

Tuesday   Date ..../........../........

Description	Amount
Total	

Wednesday   Date ..../........../........

Description	Amount
Total	

Thursday   Date ..../........../........

Description	Amount
Total	

Weekly Expense Tracker

Total Expenses : _____   **Balance :** _____

Friday
Date ……../………./……..

Description	Amount
Total	

Saturday
Date ……../………./……..

Description	Amount
Total	

Sunday
Date ……../………./……..

Description	Amount
Total	

Note

Weekly Expense Tracker

Week Of :   **Month :**   **Budget :**

Monday
Date ……../………./……..

Description	Amount
Total	

Tuesday
Date ……../………./……..

Description	Amount
Total	

Wednesday
Date ……../………./……..

Description	Amount
Total	

Thursday
Date ……../………./……..

Description	Amount
Total	

Weekly Expense Tracker

Total Expenses : _____   **Balance :** _____

Friday
Date ……../………../……..

Description	Amount
Total	

Saturday
Date ……../……../……..

Description	Amount
Total	

Sunday
Date ……../………../……..

Description	Amount
Total	

Note

_____
_____
_____
_____
_____
_____
_____
_____
_____
_____

Weekly Expense Tracker

Week Of : _____ **Month :** _____ **Budget :** _____

Monday
Date ……../……../……..

Description	Amount
Total	

Tuesday
Date ……../……../……..

Description	Amount
Total	

Wednesday
Date ……../……../……..

Description	Amount
Total	

Thursday
Date ……../……../……..

Description	Amount
Total	

Weekly Expense Tracker

Total Expenses : _____ **Balance :** _____

Friday   Date ……./………/……..

Description	Amount
Total	

Saturday   Date ……./………/……..

Description	Amount
Total	

Sunday   Date ……./………/……..

Description	Amount
Total	

Note

_____
_____
_____
_____
_____
_____
_____
_____
_____
_____

Monthly Budget

Income		
Income 1		
Income 2		
Other Income		
Total Income		

Budget :

Month :

Expenses

Bill To Be Paid	Date Due	Amount	Paid	Note
			○	
			○	
			○	
			○	
			○	
			○	
			○	
			○	
			○	
			○	
			○	
			○	
			○	
			○	
			○	
			○	
			○	
			○	
Total				

Monthly Budget

Other Expenses	Date	Amount	Note
Total			

Total Income

Total Expenses

Difference

Notes

_____
_____
_____
_____
_____
_____

Weekly Expense Tracker

Week Of :   **Month :**   **Budget :**

Monday   Date ..../.........../........

Description	Amount
Total	

Tuesday   Date ..../.........../........

Description	Amount
Total	

Wednesday   Date ..../.........../........

Description	Amount
Total	

Thursday   Date ..../.........../........

Description	Amount
Total	

Weekly Expense Tracker

Total Expenses : _____   **Balance :** _____

Friday
Date ……../………./……..

Description	Amount
Total	

Saturday
Date ……../………./……..

Description	Amount
Total	

Sunday
Date ……../………./……..

Description	Amount
Total	

Note

_____
_____
_____
_____
_____
_____
_____
_____
_____
_____

Weekly Expense Tracker

Week Of : _____   **Month :** _____   **Budget :** _____

Monday — Date ……/………/……

Description	Amount
Total	

Tuesday — Date ……/………/……

Description	Amount
Total	

Wednesday — Date ……/………/……

Description	Amount
Total	

Thursday — Date ……/………/……

Description	Amount
Total	

Weekly Expense Tracker

Total Expenses : **Balance :**

Friday
Date ……../………./………

Description	Amount
Total	

Saturday
Date ……../………./………

Description	Amount
Total	

Sunday
Date ……../………./………

Description	Amount
Total	

Note

Weekly Expense Tracker

Week Of :   **Month :**   **Budget :**

Monday   Date ……../………./……..

Description	Amount
Total	

Tuesday   Date ……../………./……..

Description	Amount
Total	

Wednesday   Date ……../………./……..

Description	Amount
Total	

Thursday   Date ……../………./……..

Description	Amount
Total	

Weekly Expense Tracker

Total Expenses : _____   **Balance :** _____

Friday   Date ……../………./……..

Description	Amount
Total	

Saturday   Date ……../……../……..

Description	Amount
Total	

Sunday   Date ……../………./……..

Description	Amount
Total	

Note

_____
_____
_____
_____
_____
_____
_____
_____
_____
_____
_____
_____

Weekly Expense Tracker

Week Of : _____   **Month :** _____   **Budget :** _____

Monday   Date ……/………/……

Description	Amount
Total	

Tuesday   Date ……/………/……

Description	Amount
Total	

Wednesday   Date ……/………/……

Description	Amount
Total	

Thursday   Date ……/………/……

Description	Amount
Total	

Weekly Expense Tracker

Total Expenses : _____   **Balance :** _____

Friday   Date ……../………./……..

Description	Amount
Total	

Saturday   Date ……../………./……..

Description	Amount
Total	

Sunday   Date ……../………./……..

Description	Amount
Total	

Note

_____
_____
_____
_____
_____
_____
_____
_____
_____
_____
_____

Weekly Expense Tracker

Week Of :　　　　　**Month :**　　　　　**Budget :**

Monday　　　　　Date ..../.........../........

Description	Amount
Total	

Tuesday　　　　　Date ..../.........../........

Description	Amount
Total	

Wednesday　　　　　Date ..../.........../........

Description	Amount
Total	

Thursday　　　　　Date ..../.........../........

Description	Amount
Total	

Weekly Expense Tracker

Total Expenses : _____   **Balance :** _____

Friday
Date ……../………../……..

Description	Amount
Total	

Saturday
Date ……../……….../………

Description	Amount
Total	

Sunday
Date ……../……….../………

Description	Amount
Total	

Note

Monthly Budget

Income		
Income 1		
Income 2		
Other Income		
Total Income		

Budget :

Month :

Expenses

Bill To Be Paid	Date Due	Amount	Paid	Note
			○	
			○	
			○	
			○	
			○	
			○	
			○	
			○	
			○	
			○	
			○	
			○	
			○	
			○	
			○	
			○	
			○	
			○	
Total				

Monthly Budget

Other Expenses	Date	Amount	Note
Total			

Total Income

Total Expenses

Difference

Notes

Weekly Expense Tracker

Week Of : _____   **Month :** _____   **Budget :** _____

Monday   Date ……/………/……

Description	Amount
Total	

Tuesday   Date ……/………/……

Description	Amount
Total	

Wednesday   Date ……/………/……

Description	Amount
Total	

Thursday   Date ……/………/……

Description	Amount
Total	

Weekly Expense Tracker

Total Expenses : **Balance :**

Friday
Date ……../…….../……..

Description	Amount
Total	

Saturday
Date ……../…….../……..

Description	Amount
Total	

Sunday
Date ……../…….../……..

Description	Amount
Total	

Note

Weekly Expense Tracker

Week Of :   **Month :**   **Budget :**

Monday
Date ..../........../........

Description	Amount
Total	

Tuesday
Date ..../........../........

Description	Amount
Total	

Wednesday
Date ..../........../........

Description	Amount
Total	

Thursday
Date ..../........../........

Description	Amount
Total	

Weekly Expense Tracker

Total Expenses : _____   **Balance :** _____

Friday
Date ……../………./……..

Description	Amount
Total	

Saturday
Date ……../……../……..

Description	Amount
Total	

Sunday
Date ……../………./……..

Description	Amount
Total	

Note

_____
_____
_____
_____
_____
_____
_____
_____
_____
_____

Weekly Expense Tracker

Week Of : _____   **Month :** _____   **Budget :** _____

Monday   Date ..../.........../.........

Description	Amount
Total	

Tuesday   Date ..../.........../.........

Description	Amount
Total	

Wednesday   Date ..../.........../.........

Description	Amount
Total	

Thursday   Date ..../.........../.........

Description	Amount
Total	

Weekly Expense Tracker

Total Expenses :　　　　　　　　　　**Balance :**

Friday
Date ……../………../……..

Description	Amount
Total	

Saturday
Date ……../……../……

Description	Amount
Total	

Sunday
Date ……../………../……..

Description	Amount
Total	

Note

Weekly Expense Tracker

Week Of :   **Month :**   **Budget :**

Monday   Date ……../………./……..

Description	Amount
Total	

Tuesday   Date ……../………./……..

Description	Amount
Total	

Wednesday   Date ……../………./……..

Description	Amount
Total	

Thursday   Date ……../………./……..

Description	Amount
Total	

Weekly Expense Tracker

Total Expenses : _____   **Balance :** _____

Friday   Date ……/……./……

Description	Amount
Total	

Saturday   Date ……/……./……

Description	Amount
Total	

Sunday   Date ……/……./……

Description	Amount
Total	

Note

Weekly Expense Tracker

Week Of :　　　　　　**Month :**　　　　　　**Budget :**

Monday　　　　Date ……../………./……..

Description	Amount
Total	

Tuesday　　　　Date ……../………./……..

Description	Amount
Total	

Wednesday　　　　Date ……../………./……..

Description	Amount
Total	

Thursday　　　　Date ……../………./……..

Description	Amount
Total	

Weekly Expense Tracker

Total Expenses : _____   **Balance :** _____

Friday   Date ……../………./……..

Description	Amount
Total	

Saturday   Date ……../……../……

Description	Amount
Total	

Sunday   Date ……../………./……..

Description	Amount
Total	

Note

_____
_____
_____
_____
_____
_____
_____
_____
_____

Monthly Budget

Income	
Income 1	
Income 2	
Other Income	
Total Income	

Budget :

Month :

Expenses

Bill To Be Paid	Date Due	Amount	Paid	Note
			○	
			○	
			○	
			○	
			○	
			○	
			○	
			○	
			○	
			○	
			○	
			○	
			○	
			○	
			○	
			○	
			○	
			○	
Total				

Monthly Budget

Other Expenses	Date	Amount	Note
Total			

Total Income

Total Expenses

Difference

Notes

Weekly Expense Tracker

Week Of : _____ **Month :** _____ **Budget :** _____

Monday
Date ……../……../……..

Description	Amount
Total	

Tuesday
Date ……../……../……..

Description	Amount
Total	

Wednesday
Date ……../……../……..

Description	Amount
Total	

Thursday
Date ……../……../……..

Description	Amount
Total	

Weekly Expense Tracker

Total Expenses : _____   **Balance :** _____

Friday   Date ……../………../……..

Description	Amount
Total	

Saturday   Date ……../……../…….

Description	Amount
Total	

Sunday   Date ……../………../……..

Description	Amount
Total	

Note

_____
_____
_____
_____
_____
_____
_____
_____
_____
_____

Weekly Expense Tracker

Week Of :　　　　　**Month :**　　　　　**Budget :**

Monday　　　Date ……../………./……..

Description	Amount
Total	

Tuesday　　　Date ……../………./……..

Description	Amount
Total	

Wednesday　　　Date ……../………./……..

Description	Amount
Total	

Thursday　　　Date ……../………./……..

Description	Amount
Total	

Weekly Expense Tracker

Total Expenses :　　　　　　　　　**Balance :**

Friday　　　　　　　Date ……../……../……..

Description	Amount
Total	

Saturday　　　　　　Date ……../……../……..

Description	Amount
Total	

Sunday　　　　　　　Date ……../……../……..

Description	Amount
Total	

Note

Weekly Expense Tracker

Week Of : **Month :** **Budget :**

Monday   Date ……/……./…….

Description	Amount
Total	

Tuesday   Date ……/……./…….

Description	Amount
Total	

Wednesday   Date ……/……./…….

Description	Amount
Total	

Thursday   Date ……/……./…….

Description	Amount
Total	

Weekly Expense Tracker

Total Expenses : _____   **Balance :** _____

Friday
Date ……../……..../……..

Description	Amount
Total	

Saturday
Date ……../……..../……..

Description	Amount
Total	

Sunday
Date ……../……..../……..

Description	Amount
Total	

Note

Weekly Expense Tracker

Week Of : _____ **Month :** _____ **Budget :** _____

Monday
Date ……../………./……..

Description	Amount
Total	

Tuesday
Date ……../……../……..

Description	Amount
Total	

Wednesday
Date ……../………./……..

Description	Amount
Total	

Thursday
Date ……../……../……..

Description	Amount
Total	

Weekly Expense Tracker

Total Expenses : _____   **Balance :** _____

Friday   Date ……../………./……..

Description	Amount
Total	

Saturday   Date ……../………./……..

Description	Amount
Total	

Sunday   Date ……../………./……..

Description	Amount
Total	

Note

_____
_____
_____
_____
_____
_____
_____
_____
_____
_____
_____

Weekly Expense Tracker

Week Of :   **Month :**   **Budget :**

Monday
Date ……../……../……..

Description	Amount
Total	

Tuesday
Date ……../……../……..

Description	Amount
Total	

Wednesday
Date ……../……../……..

Description	Amount
Total	

Thursday
Date ……../……../……..

Description	Amount
Total	

Weekly Expense Tracker

Total Expenses : **Balance :**

Friday
Date ..../........../........

Description	Amount
Total	

Saturday
Date ..../........../........

Description	Amount
Total	

Sunday
Date ..../........../........

Description	Amount
Total	

Note

Monthly Budget

Income	
Income 1	
Income 2	
Other Income	
Total Income	

Budget :

Month :

Expenses

Bill To Be Paid	Date Due	Amount	Paid	Note
			○	
			○	
			○	
			○	
			○	
			○	
			○	
			○	
			○	
			○	
			○	
			○	
			○	
			○	
			○	
			○	
			○	
			○	
Total				

Monthly Budget

Other Expenses	Date	Amount	Note
Total			

Total Income

Total Expenses

Difference

Notes

Weekly Expense Tracker

Week Of : _____ **Month :** _____ **Budget :** _____

Monday   Date ……/………/……

Description	Amount
Total	

Tuesday   Date ……/………/……

Description	Amount
Total	

Wednesday   Date ……/………/……

Description	Amount
Total	

Thursday   Date ……/………/……

Description	Amount
Total	

Weekly Expense Tracker

Total Expenses : _____   **Balance :** _____

Friday   Date ……./………./……..

Description	Amount
Total	

Saturday   Date ……./………./……..

Description	Amount
Total	

Sunday   Date ……./………./……..

Description	Amount
Total	

Note

_____
_____
_____
_____
_____
_____
_____
_____
_____
_____

Weekly Expense Tracker

Week Of :   **Month :**   **Budget :**

Monday
Date ……../………./……..

Description	Amount
Total	

Tuesday
Date ……../………./……..

Description	Amount
Total	

Wednesday
Date ……../………./……..

Description	Amount
Total	

Thursday
Date ……../………./……..

Description	Amount
Total	

Weekly Expense Tracker

Total Expenses : _____ **Balance :** _____

Friday   Date ……./………./……..

Description	Amount
Total	

Saturday   Date ……./……../…….

Description	Amount
Total	

Sunday   Date ……./………./……..

Description	Amount
Total	

Note

_____
_____
_____
_____
_____
_____
_____
_____
_____
_____
_____
_____

Weekly Expense Tracker

Week Of : _____   **Month :** _____   **Budget :** _____

Monday   Date ……../………./……..

Description	Amount
Total	

Tuesday   Date ……../………./……..

Description	Amount
Total	

Wednesday   Date ……../………./……..

Description	Amount
Total	

Thursday   Date ……../………./……..

Description	Amount
Total	

Weekly Expense Tracker

Total Expenses : _____   **Balance :** _____

Friday   Date ……../………../……..

Description	Amount
Total	

Saturday   Date ……../………../……..

Description	Amount
Total	

Sunday   Date ……../………../……..

Description	Amount
Total	

Note

_____
_____
_____
_____
_____
_____
_____
_____
_____
_____
_____
_____
_____

Weekly Expense Tracker

Week Of :　　　　　　**Month :**　　　　　　**Budget :**

Monday　　　Date ……./…….../……..

Description	Amount
Total	

Tuesday　　　Date ……./…….../……..

Description	Amount
Total	

Wednesday　　　Date ……./…….../……..

Description	Amount
Total	

Thursday　　　Date ……./…….../……..

Description	Amount
Total	

Weekly Expense Tracker

Total Expenses :   **Balance :**

Friday   Date ……../………./……..

Description	Amount
Total	

Saturday   Date ……../………./……..

Description	Amount
Total	

Sunday   Date ……../………./……..

Description	Amount
Total	

Note

Weekly Expense Tracker

Week Of : _____ **Month :** _____ **Budget :** _____

Monday   Date ……/……../……..

Description	Amount
Total	

Tuesday   Date ……/……../……..

Description	Amount
Total	

Wednesday   Date ……/……../……..

Description	Amount
Total	

Thursday   Date ……/……../……..

Description	Amount
Total	

Weekly Expense Tracker

Total Expenses : **Balance :**

Friday   Date ……./……../……..

Description	Amount
Total	

Saturday   Date ……./……../……

Description	Amount
Total	

Sunday   Date ……./……../……..

Description	Amount
Total	

Note

Monthly Budget

Income	
Income 1	
Income 2	
Other Income	
Total Income	

Budget :

Month :

Expenses

Bill To Be Paid	Date Due	Amount	Paid	Note
			○	
			○	
			○	
			○	
			○	
			○	
			○	
			○	
			○	
			○	
			○	
			○	
			○	
			○	
			○	
			○	
			○	
			○	
Total				

Monthly Budget

Other Expenses	Date	Amount	Note
Total			

Total Income

Total Expenses

Difference

Notes

Weekly Expense Tracker

Week Of : **Month :** **Budget :**

Monday   Date ……../………../……..

Description	Amount
Total	

Tuesday   Date ……../………../……..

Description	Amount
Total	

Wednesday   Date ……../………../……..

Description	Amount
Total	

Thursday   Date ……../………../……..

Description	Amount
Total	

Weekly Expense Tracker

Total Expenses : _____   **Balance :** _____

Friday
Date ……../………../……..

Description	Amount
Total	

Saturday
Date ……../………../……..

Description	Amount
Total	

Sunday
Date ……../………../……..

Description	Amount
Total	

Note

_____
_____
_____
_____
_____
_____
_____
_____
_____
_____
_____

Weekly Expense Tracker

Week Of : _____ **Month :** _____ **Budget :** _____

Monday   Date ……/……../……..

Description	Amount
Total	

Tuesday   Date ……/……../……..

Description	Amount
Total	

Wednesday   Date ……/……../……..

Description	Amount
Total	

Thursday   Date ……/……../……..

Description	Amount
Total	

Weekly Expense Tracker

Total Expenses : _____   **Balance :** _____

Friday   Date ……../………../……..

Description	Amount
Total	

Saturday   Date ……../………../……..

Description	Amount
Total	

Sunday   Date ……../………../……..

Description	Amount
Total	

Note

_____
_____
_____
_____
_____
_____
_____
_____
_____
_____
_____

Weekly Expense Tracker

Week Of : **Month :** **Budget :**

Monday
Date ..../.........../........

Description	Amount
Total	

Tuesday
Date ..../.........../........

Description	Amount
Total	

Wednesday
Date ..../.........../........

Description	Amount
Total	

Thursday
Date ..../.........../........

Description	Amount
Total	

Weekly Expense Tracker

Total Expenses : _____ **Balance :** _____

Friday Date ……/……../……..

Description	Amount
Total	

Saturday Date ……/……../……..

Description	Amount
Total	

Sunday Date ……/……../……..

Description	Amount
Total	

Note

_____
_____
_____
_____
_____
_____
_____
_____
_____
_____
_____

Weekly Expense Tracker

Week Of : _____   **Month :** _____   **Budget :** _____

Monday   Date ..../........./.......

Description	Amount
Total	

Tuesday   Date ..../........./.......

Description	Amount
Total	

Wednesday   Date ..../........./.......

Description	Amount
Total	

Thursday   Date ..../........./.......

Description	Amount
Total	

Weekly Expense Tracker

Total Expenses : _____   **Balance :** _____

Friday
Date ……../……….../……..

Description	Amount
Total	

Saturday
Date ……../……../……

Description	Amount
Total	

Sunday
Date ……../……….../……..

Description	Amount
Total	

Note

_____
_____
_____
_____
_____
_____
_____
_____
_____
_____

Weekly Expense Tracker

Week Of : _____   **Month :** _____   **Budget :** _____

Monday — Date ……./………./…….

Description	Amount
Total	

Tuesday — Date ……./………./…….

Description	Amount
Total	

Wednesday — Date ……./………./…….

Description	Amount
Total	

Thursday — Date ……./………./…….

Description	Amount
Total	

Weekly Expense Tracker

Total Expenses : _____ **Balance :** _____

Friday
Date ……../………./……..

Description	Amount
Total	

Saturday
Date ……../……../……

Description	Amount
Total	

Sunday
Date ……../………./……..

Description	Amount
Total	

Note

_____
_____
_____
_____
_____
_____
_____
_____
_____
_____
_____
_____

Monthly Budget

Income		
Income 1		
Income 2		
Other Income		
Total Income		

Budget :

Month :

Expenses

Bill To Be Paid	Date Due	Amount	Paid	Note
			○	
			○	
			○	
			○	
			○	
			○	
			○	
			○	
			○	
			○	
			○	
			○	
			○	
			○	
			○	
			○	
			○	
			○	
Total				

Monthly Budget

Other Expenses	Date	Amount	Note
Total			

Total Income

Total Expenses

Difference

Notes

Weekly Expense Tracker

Week Of :   **Month :**   **Budget :**

Monday
Date ..../........../........

Description	Amount
Total	

Tuesday
Date ..../........../........

Description	Amount
Total	

Wednesday
Date ..../........../........

Description	Amount
Total	

Thursday
Date ..../........../........

Description	Amount
Total	

Weekly Expense Tracker

Total Expenses :　　　　　　　　**Balance :**

Friday　　　　　　**Date** ……../………./……..

Description	Amount
Total	

Saturday　　　　　**Date** ……../……../…….

Description	Amount
Total	

Sunday　　　　　　**Date** ……../………./……..

Description	Amount
Total	

Note

Weekly Expense Tracker

Week Of : _____ **Month :** _____ **Budget :** _____

Monday
Date ..../........../........

Description	Amount
Total	

Tuesday
Date ..../........../........

Description	Amount
Total	

Wednesday
Date ..../........../........

Description	Amount
Total	

Thursday
Date ..../........../........

Description	Amount
Total	

Weekly Expense Tracker

Total Expenses :   **Balance :**

Friday   Date ……../………../……..

Description	Amount
Total	

Saturday   Date ……../……../…….

Description	Amount
Total	

Sunday   Date ……../………../……..

Description	Amount
Total	

Note

_____
_____
_____
_____
_____
_____
_____
_____
_____
_____
_____
_____

Weekly Expense Tracker

Week Of : _____ **Month :** _____ **Budget :** _____

Monday
Date ..../........../........

Description	Amount
Total	

Tuesday
Date ..../........./........

Description	Amount
Total	

Wednesday
Date ..../........../........

Description	Amount
Total	

Thursday
Date ..../........./........

Description	Amount
Total	

Weekly Expense Tracker

Total Expenses :　　　　　　　　　**Balance :**

Friday　　　　　　　　Date
……../………./……..

Description	Amount
Total	

Saturday　　　　　　　Date
……../………./……..

Description	Amount
Total	

Sunday　　　　　　　　Date
……../………./……..

Description	Amount
Total	

Note

Weekly Expense Tracker

Week Of : _____ **Month :** _____ **Budget :** _____

Monday
Date ..../........../........

Description	Amount
Total	

Tuesday
Date ..../........../........

Description	Amount
Total	

Wednesday
Date ..../........../........

Description	Amount
Total	

Thursday
Date ..../........../........

Description	Amount
Total	

Weekly Expense Tracker

Total Expenses : _____   **Balance :** _____

Friday
Date ……../………../……..

Description	Amount
Total	

Saturday
Date ……../………../……..

Description	Amount
Total	

Sunday
Date ……../………../……..

Description	Amount
Total	

Note

_____
_____
_____
_____
_____
_____
_____
_____
_____
_____
_____

Weekly Expense Tracker

Week Of :   **Month :**   **Budget :**

Monday
Date ……../………./……..

Description	Amount
Total	

Tuesday
Date ……../………./……..

Description	Amount
Total	

Wednesday
Date ……../………./……..

Description	Amount
Total	

Thursday
Date ……../………./……..

Description	Amount
Total	

Weekly Expense Tracker

Total Expenses : _____   **Balance :** _____

Friday   Date ……./……../……..

Description	Amount
Total	

Saturday   Date ……./……../……..

Description	Amount
Total	

Sunday   Date ……./……../……..

Description	Amount
Total	

Note

_____
_____
_____
_____
_____
_____
_____
_____
_____
_____
_____
_____

Monthly Budget

Income		
Income 1		
Income 2		
Other Income		
Total Income		

Budget :

Month :

Expenses

Bill To Be Paid	Date Due	Amount	Paid	Note
			○	
			○	
			○	
			○	
			○	
			○	
			○	
			○	
			○	
			○	
			○	
			○	
			○	
			○	
			○	
			○	
			○	
			○	
			○	
Total				

Monthly Budget

Other Expenses	Date	Amount	Note
Total			

Total Income

Total Expenses

Difference

Notes

Weekly Expense Tracker

Week Of :   **Month :**   **Budget :**

Monday   Date ..../........../........

Description	Amount
Total	

Tuesday   Date ..../........../........

Description	Amount
Total	

Wednesday   Date ..../........../........

Description	Amount
Total	

Thursday   Date ..../........../........

Description	Amount
Total	

Weekly Expense Tracker

Total Expenses : _____   **Balance :** _____

Friday   Date ……../……….../……..

Description	Amount
Total	

Saturday   Date ……../……….../……..

Description	Amount
Total	

Sunday   Date ……../……….../……..

Description	Amount
Total	

Note

_____
_____
_____
_____
_____
_____
_____
_____
_____
_____

Weekly Expense Tracker

Week Of : _____ **Month :** _____ **Budget :** _____

Monday — Date ……../……..../……..

Description	Amount
Total	

Tuesday — Date ……../……..../……..

Description	Amount
Total	

Wednesday — Date ……../……..../……..

Description	Amount
Total	

Thursday — Date ……../……..../……..

Description	Amount
Total	

Weekly Expense Tracker

Total Expenses : _____   **Balance :** _____

Friday   Date ……../………./……..

Description	Amount
Total	

Saturday   Date ……../………./……..

Description	Amount
Total	

Sunday   Date ……../………./……..

Description	Amount
Total	

Note

_____
_____
_____
_____
_____
_____
_____
_____
_____
_____

Weekly Expense Tracker

Week Of : _____ **Month :** _____ **Budget :** _____

Monday
Date ..../........../........

Description	Amount
Total	

Tuesday
Date ..../........../........

Description	Amount
Total	

Wednesday
Date ..../........../........

Description	Amount
Total	

Thursday
Date ..../........../........

Description	Amount
Total	

Weekly Expense Tracker

Total Expenses : _____   **Balance :** _____

Friday
Date ……../……….../……..

Description	Amount
Total	

Saturday
Date ……../……….../……..

Description	Amount
Total	

Sunday
Date ……../……….../……..

Description	Amount
Total	

Note

_____
_____
_____
_____
_____
_____
_____
_____
_____
_____

Weekly Expense Tracker

Week Of : **Month :** **Budget :**

Monday
Date ..../............/........

Description	Amount
Total	

Tuesday
Date ..../............/........

Description	Amount
Total	

Wednesday
Date ..../............/........

Description	Amount
Total	

Thursday
Date ..../............/........

Description	Amount
Total	

Weekly Expense Tracker

Total Expenses : _____ **Balance :** _____

Friday
Date ……./………./……..

Description	Amount
Total	

Saturday
Date ……./………./……..

Description	Amount
Total	

Sunday
Date ……./………./……..

Description	Amount
Total	

Note

_____
_____
_____
_____
_____
_____
_____
_____
_____
_____
_____
_____

Weekly Expense Tracker

Week Of : _____ **Month :** _____ **Budget :** _____

Monday
Date ……../………../……..

Description	Amount
Total	

Tuesday
Date ……../………../……..

Description	Amount
Total	

Wednesday
Date ……../………../……..

Description	Amount
Total	

Thursday
Date ……../………../……..

Description	Amount
Total	

Weekly Expense Tracker

Total Expenses : _____   **Balance :** _____

Friday   Date ……./………./……..

Description	Amount
Total	

Saturday   Date ……./………./……..

Description	Amount
Total	

Sunday   Date ……./………./……..

Description	Amount
Total	

Note

_____
_____
_____
_____
_____
_____
_____
_____
_____
_____
_____

Monthly Budget

Income		
Income 1		
Income 2		
Other Income		
Total Income		

Budget :

Month :

Expenses

Bill To Be Paid	Date Due	Amount	Paid	Note
			○	
			○	
			○	
			○	
			○	
			○	
			○	
			○	
			○	
			○	
			○	
			○	
			○	
			○	
			○	
			○	
			○	
			○	
			○	
Total				

Monthly Budget

Other Expenses	Date	Amount	Note
Total			

Total Income

Total Expenses

Difference

Notes

Weekly Expense Tracker

Week Of :　　　　　**Month :**　　　　　　　**Budget :**

Monday
Date ……../………./……..

Description	Amount
Total	

Tuesday
Date ……../………./……..

Description	Amount
Total	

Wednesday
Date ……../………./……..

Description	Amount
Total	

Thursday
Date ……../………./……..

Description	Amount
Total	

Weekly Expense Tracker

Total Expenses : _____   **Balance :** _____

Friday   Date ……../…..…../……..

Description	Amount
Total	

Saturday   Date ……../…..…../……..

Description	Amount
Total	

Sunday   Date ……../…..…../……..

Description	Amount
Total	

Note

_____
_____
_____
_____
_____
_____
_____
_____
_____
_____

Weekly Expense Tracker

Week Of :   **Month :**   **Budget :**

Monday
Date ……../……….../……..

Description	Amount
Total	

Tuesday
Date ……../……….../……..

Description	Amount
Total	

Wednesday
Date ……../……….../……..

Description	Amount
Total	

Thursday
Date ……../……….../……..

Description	Amount
Total	

Weekly Expense Tracker

Total Expenses : _____   **Balance :** _____

Friday
Date ……./………./……..

Description	Amount
Total	

Saturday
Date ……./………/………

Description	Amount
Total	

Sunday
Date ……./………./……..

Description	Amount
Total	

Note

_____
_____
_____
_____
_____
_____
_____
_____
_____
_____

Weekly Expense Tracker

Week Of : _____ **Month :** _____ **Budget :** _____

Monday
Date ……../……….../……..

Description	Amount
Total	

Tuesday
Date ……../……….../……..

Description	Amount
Total	

Wednesday
Date ……../……….../……..

Description	Amount
Total	

Thursday
Date ……../……….../……..

Description	Amount
Total	

Weekly Expense Tracker

Total Expenses : _____ **Balance :** _____

Friday Date ……/………/……..

Description	Amount
Total	

Saturday Date ……/………/……..

Description	Amount
Total	

Sunday Date ……/………/……..

Description	Amount
Total	

Note

_____
_____
_____
_____
_____
_____
_____
_____
_____
_____
_____
_____
_____

Weekly Expense Tracker

Week Of :   **Month :**   **Budget :**

Monday   Date ……../………../……..

Description	Amount
Total	

Tuesday   Date ……../………../……..

Description	Amount
Total	

Wednesday   Date ……../………../……..

Description	Amount
Total	

Thursday   Date ……../………../……..

Description	Amount
Total	

Weekly Expense Tracker

Total Expenses :   **Balance :**

Friday   Date ……../………./……..

Description	Amount
Total	

Saturday   Date ……../………/………

Description	Amount
Total	

Sunday   Date ……../………./……..

Description	Amount
Total	

Note

Weekly Expense Tracker

Week Of :   **Month :**   **Budget :**

Monday
Date ……../……….../……..

Description	Amount
Total	

Tuesday
Date ……../……….../……..

Description	Amount
Total	

Wednesday
Date ……../……….../……..

Description	Amount
Total	

Thursday
Date ……../……….../……..

Description	Amount
Total	

Weekly Expense Tracker

Total Expenses : _____   **Balance :** _____

Friday   Date ……./……../……..

Description	Amount
Total	

Saturday   Date ……./……../……..

Description	Amount
Total	

Sunday   Date ……./……../……..

Description	Amount
Total	

Note

_____
_____
_____
_____
_____
_____
_____
_____
_____
_____

Made in the USA
Lexington, KY
02 July 2019